THE MINDSET NEEDED FOR BUSINESS SUCCESS

CONTENTS

DISCLAIMER NOTICE

Despite making every effort to be as accurate and thorough as possible, the Publisher does not at any time guarantee or represent that the contents of this report are correct due to the Internet's tendency to change quickly.

Although every effort has been taken to verify the content in this publication, the Publisher disclaims all liability for any mistakes, omissions, or other interpretations of the subject matter. Any perceived slights towards particular people, groups, or organizations are accidental.

This book offers a practical guide to online marketing. Like everything else in life, there are no guarantees of income made in books with practical advice.

Readers are advised to respond based on their own judgment regarding their own circumstances and take appropriate action.

This book is not meant to be a source for accounting, financial, legal, or business advice. All readers are urged to consult with qualified experts in the fields of law, business, accounting, and finance.

Printing this book for easier reading is advised.

WHY DO INTERNET STARTUPS FAIL SO FREQUENTLY NOW?

Every day, millions upon millions of people pull themselves from their warm, warm beds, take a shower, grab a cup of coffee, and make their way to their work with the belief that there must be a simpler way to earn a living.

Every single one of those billions of individuals knows someone who has given up the daily grind of getting up and going to work in order to work from home on their personal computers and earn a very nice salary.

To them, working from home seems like the perfect option. Many of these unsatisfied individuals would quit their professions and dive into internet marketing without any training, preparation, or education in the field, and with no chance of success. They are doomed to failure, but they haven't even considered it.

The truth is that more than 90% (ninety percent) of all Internet business startups fail within the first 120 days, according to numerous statistics. You did read that correctly. EIGHTY NINE PERCENT!

This failure rate ought to serve as a cautionary tale for anyone thinking about attempting to succeed working online rather than in a traditional employment.

Success is certainly a possibility. There ARE those other 10% (10%) who actually succeed. Success doesn't happen by chance, that's the thing. Success is also not merely a matter of chance. Success is the result of a number of crucial variables.

Success is a result of people's correct conceptions about internet marketing's operation. They don't anticipate becoming instantly wealthy or being able to make a killing over night so they can go to a tropical island.

Strangely enough, the same folks who wouldn't dream of beginning a real-world business somehow believe they can succeed with an online business despite having no prior experience in the field.

People will start an online business with the expectation that they won't need to get up and commute to work anymore. They believe that as long as they only work when they feel like it, they can still live comfortably. They simply do not anticipate having to put in a lot of effort or stay up late.

Internet stereotypes that are incorrect

When you consider the people who are launching internet enterprises, the 90% failure rate of new businesses is actually not that shocking.

For some reason, the majority of individuals believe that starting a successful online business only requires building a website and posting a "open for business" sign. They are completely mistaken.

Any type of successful online company takes self-discipline.

Many people who start an online business believe they can work three to four hours in front of a computer, party all night, sleep until noon, and then earn a living.

They seem to believe that everyone will simply gather on their website and donate money. It will not take place.

Internet companies don't operate automatically. While it is true that established internet marketing experts don't need to work long, arduous hours on their businesses, this privilege has only been granted after many long, arduous hours.

They didn't experience it overnight, and no one else will either.

The majority of people are completely unprepared for the time commitment required to launch a successful online business.

NO BUSINESS EXPERIENCE

Two things apply to all businesses. They must be managed like businesses because they are! The people in control of a company must be aware of standard business procedures.

They must comprehend fundamental concepts like allowable overhead costs in proportion to predicted revenue. Internet business owners must comprehend profit and loss and what each entails.

An internet company entrepreneur does not need need a business degree to succeed, although it certainly wouldn't hurt. Even the most fundamental understanding of business is crucial.

Keep your day job and put off beginning an online business if you have trouble keeping track of your personal finances.

While it's true that you can pay accounting firms to provide you with information such as the WHEN of tax deposits, these businesses cannot inform you of the NEED for such deposits.

Accounting firms can tell you if you made a profit or not, but they cannot tell you how to make one. Before you even consider starting an online business if you have no prior business experience, you need, at the absolute least, seek some sound business counsel.

The truth is that good business principles underlie all prosperous enterprises.

Successful companies don't just happen. Only 10% of new internet enterprises are profitable or even remain in operation after their first 120 days of operation, as shown by the data.

For many, many months, it is not even fair to anticipate turning a profit from a new business venture.

You must have enough money on hand to both start your business and meet your personal demands for a considerable amount of time. There is no getting around the necessity for enough of what is known as "capital."

THERE JUST ISN'T THE RIGHT MINDSET!

Most certainly, you've heard the expression "He has an attitude!" This is typically used to make fun of someone who has a bad attitude.

But when talking about start-ups in internet marketing, the word "attitude" is crucial. A positive attitude and a positive mindset cannot ensure success, but a negative attitude and a negative mindset can almost surely do so.

Here are several unfavorable attitudes that will ensure failure:

1. I am able to work when I wish. False, false, false! Working whenever you feel like it is not an option. In order to create a new online business, you must be prepared to labor many long, arduous hours.

2. I'll quickly get wealthy! You could not be more mistaken, and not only are you mistaken but you are also endangering yourself. If you're seeking for a quick method to get money, you ARE the next target because there are countless con artists on the internet looking for their next easy victim.

With internet marketing businesses, it is possible to earn a very comfortable income, but if someone ever claims it is quick or easy, they are lying to you.

3. A business plan is not necessary. Once more, you are incorrect. Online commerce is still commerce. Online businesses must adhere to the same ethical standards as traditional brick and mortar ones. You must have a strategy for achievement that is founded on these good business concepts.

4. You don't have a boss when you run your own online business. Mistake again! Your boss is you. You will consign yourself to failure if you aren't a good boss who ensures that job is completed fully and on schedule. You will likely find yourself working in a job under a boss who

does such things, possibly at minimum salary, unless you are one who puts up a working schedule and makes goals that must be accomplished.

HOW TO STAY AWAY FROM THE FAILING MASSES

The thing about launching a business, any business, is that there is never a guarantee of success.

Even large, global corporations are capable of failing when trying something new. Although there is always a chance of failure, the likelihood of success can be increased.

Enhancing your chances of success entails:

1. **Having a strong business strategy in place PRIOR to starting your online venture** "Those who fail to plan, plan to fail," goes an old adage. It is necessary to have a comprehensive set of success plans. You must have a detailed list of the steps required to get from point A to point B, together with reasonable cost projections for completing each step.

2. **Expecting to put in a lot of effort to reach your objectives.** Never assume everything will be simple. Most of the time, you will be correct because nothing is ever as simple as it seems. Each step on the path to success needs effort, persistence, and time. On occasion, things don't turn out as planned the first time. You must be prepared to attempt once more and again until you succeed.

3. **Avoiding "get wealthy quick" scams**. There are many people who prey on people looking for quick and simple solutions to get rich online. These approaches don't exist. Stop believing there is a simple solution. NOT; there is.

Keep in mind those figures! In the first 120 days, 90% of all new online enterprises fail. You are not required to belong to that majority. You may join the 10% minority of prosperous internet business ventures.

The Foundations of a Successful Internet Business

When you are on the outside looking in, operating a successful internet business can seem quite easy. A wealthy internet business owner doesn't appear to be doing anything exceptional, but he is clearly enjoying life. He doesn't appear to be exerting himself all that much. He seemed to be having a great time.

Really, all he does is spend a few hours each day relaxing in front of his own computer in his own cozy house. He speaks on the phone and appears to enjoy each exchange.

Evidently, operating a prosperous online business is a "piece of cake"! Right? WRONG!!! False, false, false!

You are seeing the end result of a very, very laborious process that took many years and involved many late-night hours and a lot of blood, sweat, and tears.

This successful internet business owner put in a ton of effort to get the success you are seeing.

In the long process of constructing his prosperous Internet firm, it is more than a little possible that he first laid four cornerstones. These four pillars are the foundation upon which he built his success.

2. Understanding and applying leverage.

3. Creating a network of beneficial contacts.

4. He most likely had a mentor as well.

We will talk about these four cornerstones that must be established initially in order to build a successful online business.

All of these are critical to the success of any business, but especially the success of an online business. They are all important.

There are many aspects of developing a successful online business that are similar to those of building a successful brick and mortar firm, but there are also important differences.

Any business, whether it be online or offline, needs to start off with the appropriate mindset if it wants to succeed.

While having a positive, healthy perspective won't ensure success, having a negative, unhealthy, or unrealistic thinking will almost certainly do so. In order to build a successful business, the first cornerstone that must be established is the proper mindset.

What does a good, healthy mindset entail? Both things that it is and things that it isn't are true.

The determination to work as hard and as long as is necessary to accomplish the goals that have been established IS a proper and healthy mindset. A healthy and positive outlook DOES NOT hold the idea that success will be simple, fast, or painless.

People who think they can successfully run an online business without investing any time or effort are destined to fail from the start.

There are con artists and scammers lurking on internet, waiting impatiently for people hoping for quick money to show up.

The willingness to invest the time necessary to create a decent company plan based on sound business principles is a sign of a right and healthy attitude.

A healthy and appropriate mindset DON'T simply dive in head first and hope for the best. In those conditions, the best that can happen is that you escape with more than two cents in your pocket.

In the realm of online marketing, "flying by the seat of your trousers" is just not an option. If you don't have a formal education in business, you should seek out those who do and pay attention to their advise.

UTILIZING AND UNDERSTANDING LEVERAGE

There are dozens, perhaps hundreds, of different company models. Of course, some are more successful than others, but each has advantages and disadvantages of their own.

The goal is to maximize your investment. If you want your e-business to be successful, you must harness the full potential of the Internet. You simply can't afford to overlook anything.

If you are a true go-getter, you may be tempted to complete every task first, but that is impossible. Create a realistic plan, then build on it until you have a strong foundation from which to operate.

Once you have a website up and running, you must use SEO (search engine optimization) to raise your page rank.

Of course, one thing often leads to another, but adding a blog to your website is one of the easiest methods to benefit from SEO. You can use this to help the search engines index your website much more quickly.

Branding yourself, your website, and your products are all part of leveraging. Purchasing PLR (Private Label Rights) products and modifying the names of those products to add your own name or logo is one of the quickest methods to start building your brand. (Remember that there needs to be some reworking.)

This is most likely the easiest way to establish a brand and credibility online. For instance, you might purchase a PLR E-Book about simple dog training and rename it "John Doe's Simple Dog Training Methods."

The book can be purchased, offered as a freebie on your website, or listed in E-Book repositories for public use.

Keep in mind that on the internet, credibility and reputation are essential. Take no quick cuts, and never harm yourself or others by doing so.

WHO YOU KNOW IS MORE IMPORTANT THAN WHAT YOU KNOW

That is a proverb. "Who you know matters more than what you know."

Building a successful e-enterprise requires laying the foundation of good, solid partnerships.

Every minute spent working hard to establish strong business relationships is time well spent. One of your key priorities should be developing business relationships.

You enter social circumstances where you interact with people who share or complement your interests when you are forming social connections, don't you, when you do that.

Inexactly the same process is used to develop business ties. You introduce yourself into professional settings where you will encounter others who run firms that are complementary to or comparable to your own. The formation of connections takes time.

There are numerous ways to complete this assignment. Participating in webinars or teleseminars that are relevant to your line of work is one option.

Naturally, you will pick up a lot of knowledge, but perhaps more crucially, you will meet people who are already successful in the specialized sector you are working in.

It goes without saying that going to live, in-person seminars is the best approach to start forming good business ties with your peers and people who can actually help you.

Which takes me to the last foundational stone you need to set.

LOCATE A COMPETENT MENTOR

A good and capable mentor is probably the most useful resource a fledgling e-entrepreneur can have. You can avoid making all of the mistakes yourself by getting assistance from someone who has already done it.

They can assist you avoid traps and guide you toward the wisest decisions since they have the wisdom that comes from experience.

You might wonder why someone with everything they need would take the effort to assist a novice in succeeding.

Maybe by telling you about my friend who is a talented musician, I can give you an answer to it. He performed alongside some of the top names in the industry. He is currently in his 70s and a very, very great guitarist.

He spends a lot of time not only teaching how to play the guitar to his three or so young students, but also giving them professional advice.

He said, "It is like earning immortality," when I questioned him about why he spent so much time doing it. What I know will live on forever if I teach them, and they in turn teach others.

The "immortality" that successful online marketers seek is also desirable. Surprisingly, the people who are the most successful are also the people who are most inclined to mentor a budding e-entrepreneur.

Naturally, these accomplished online marketer are not going to want to waste their time on someone who has not previously put a lot of effort into laying those first three cornerstones themselves.

These potential mentors are seeking for newcomers who can demonstrate that they have a positive and healthy mindset, who are committed to learning how to leverage, and who understand how crucial it is to know all the players and the RIGHT individuals.

In other words, the newcomer who is already working hard and helping himself and not searching for someone who will just smooth the road for him is the one who is most likely to acquire a mentor.

THE SECRET TO CONSTANT GROWTH AND EXTENSION

Live or die! This is a natural law that holds true for all living things. This rule also applies to all business. A company cannot start, develop to a particular size, and then stop there and keep growing.

Growth and expansion are essential for a company to thrive, and if they do not take place, the company will either fade away or crash and burn.

The owners or managers of the business must maintain control over its growth and expansion. The company falls behind the competition if growth is too slow. If a business grows too quickly, it could easily become overextended.

The optimal growth is constant and under control. The ideal and the reality are, of course, occasionally two quite different things.

It's not uncommon for people to misunderstand the phrases "growth" and "expansion." Growing larger and broader is the most obvious meaning of these words, but they are not the only ones that apply.

For instance, expansion might entail extending a company's knowledge base, while growth can mean learning new things and getting wiser.

A small internet-based firm does not need to grow and expand until it becomes a massive, multinational corporation in order to survive, but its owners and management must develop by becoming smarter and by being open to change.

Nothing merely remains the same. The only thing in life that is guaranteed is change. What was popular or successful yesterday is out of date today and will be history tomorrow.

On the internet, changes happen far more quickly than they do in the real world, which means that businesses, business owners, and company managers must evolve along with and adapt to changes as they happen.

We can all agree that for any business to survive—possibly even more so for online businesses—it must constantly evolve, adapt, and grow. Therefore, the issue is: What is the secret to the development and growth of internet-based businesses?

When physical businesses develop and expand, they construct larger premises and hire additional staff, but that isn't really an option for online enterprises.

An internet-based business's owner or manager must consistently and continually invest in it if it is to develop and expand.

They must be prepared to stay up to date with technology and to embrace and accommodate changes as they come about.

Businesses on the internet are not structures. People run online enterprises. By putting money into a bigger building, an online firm cannot expand.

It only develops when the individual in charge of that business makes an investment in their own expertise.

By spending money on recruiting more employees, an online firm cannot grow. When the person running an online business invests in themselves, their business grows.

The bottom line is that investing continuously in the business owner or management is the key to the ongoing growth and expansion of an internet-based firm. The gist of it is: Invest in yourself.

INVEST IN YOURSELF

This refrain has probably been repeated a lot to you.

"Make an investment in yourself! Put your self first! What does it mean, though, to "invest in yourself"? Does that suggest you should invest in a $200 haircut right away? Does this imply that you need to buy a designer outfit on your own? How should you define self-investment?

However, that is not the type of investment we are discussing here. If you can afford it, go get that haircut and buy that fancy suit.

Your internet business only requires a computer, an internet connection, and you to run it from anywhere on the earth that has access to the internet.

Therefore, your company essentially consists of only you. Only your expertise and skill are the foundation of your business. These are the "company" assets, and in order for your online business to succeed, they must continuously grow and expand.

Here is a guideline you might wish to follow to ensure the success and longevity of your online business: Spend 5% of your time and money on yourself to get better.

In order to survive, an internet business must expand and grow, and for that to happen, the person in charge of that operation—that would be YOU—must also expand and grow their own expertise.

You can ensure that you continue to have great financial returns for a very long time by making a very small investment in yourself each year— just 5% of your time and income.

What is meant by a 5% time and income investment per year in yourself may still have you scratching your head as you sit there. You need to increase your knowledge, is what is intended.

It's important to keep up with new technology developments and to broaden your knowledge in your field of expertise. Things shift quickly. Every day of the week, new knowledge on practically everything under the sun becomes available.

Falling behind quickly is a very, very easy process. And if you don't make a conscious effort to stay on top of things, you will undoubtedly lag behind.

Catching up is more difficult; nevertheless, if you keep up, you can generally find a way to move ahead.

Yes, you are currently so busy that you could utilize 48 hours per day, but investing just a little bit of time and money—roughly an hour per day out of the 24 that you are allowed and $5 from every $100 you make—into yourself now will double your earnings by a hundred.

There are newsletters, webinars, teleseminars, and actual brick and mortar seminars that can provide information and help your knowledge grow and expand so that your business can also grow and expand, but you must be willing to invest in yourself in order to take advantage of this information, learn from it, and apply it to your own online business.

TIPS FOR SELF-INVESTMENT THAT REALLY WORK

It is unquestionably true that the one resource that the majority of online business owners are severely lacking is time. There are still methods for investing in yourself using time that might otherwise be useless. The following advice could be helpful:

Invest in yourself throughout your journey time. You can use the time you spend traveling to learn more by using your iPod or MP3 player.

☐ A half-hour earlier time setting will allow you to read and learn throughout that period.

☐ Use your computer to look for fresh facts and concepts after work in the evening.

Of course, there are some things that will merely require time, but you can make a good decision.

Attend webinars and teleseminars that are specifically about your industry or company.

Attend practical seminars that are close to your house, will save you time traveling, and will provide you the knowledge you need.

AVOID THE TEMPTATION TO STAY IN YOUR COMFORT ZONE

Each of us has a personal comfort zone, which we all love very much. It is very, very tempting to continue doing things the same way we always have and to only change the little details.

However, failing to leave your comfort zone and refuse to broaden your thoughts and horizons may lead to the failure of both your online business and you.

If it ain't broke, don't fix it, goes an ancient adage that was probably coined by someone who was hesitant to attempt new things. Whatever "it" is, it doesn't necessarily need to be broken in order to be better.

Although the candlelight wasn't destroyed, we are all happy that electricity was created.

Even while electric light is still light, it is unquestionably an enormous improvement over candlelight.

In the field of online business, new concepts emerge every day. Even though they are outside of our personal comfort zones, some of those ideas are actually wonderful ones.

You must be prepared to step outside of your comfort zone if you want to continue investing in yourself. There may still be newer, better, and more effective ways to accomplish goals just because what has previously worked continues to do so.

Nobody asserts that something new is always better. Even while new ideas aren't always superior, there are occasions when they are, and the only way to know for sure is to research new concepts on your own before using the ones that would benefit your company.

Increase your knowledge as an investment in yourself, and don't be hesitant to attempt new things and unconventional approaches. These things are the true keys to success, not just in the field of online commerce but also in general.

WORK VS. DEALS: THE RAZOR EDGE DIFFERENCE

Prior to beginning their careers in internet marketing, almost every internet marketer I have ever met held a profession that was unrelated to the industry.

Working a job where you are paid for your efforts is amusing in certain ways.

You start to think that working means making money. Working for someone else does, after all, equate to earning money.

However, if you start a profession in internet marketing, the "job" that once brought in money for you no longer brings in money.

It's true. Your current "job," which includes taking calls, responding to emails, filing paperwork, and other tasks for which you used to be paid, actually keeps you from pursuing business opportunities that will increase your income.

Nevertheless, we keep looking for job because we've been conditioned to believe that it's what generates income.

We frequently get into the trap of believing that work equals money, which is actually detrimental to developing a profitable internet marketing firm.

Instead of concentrating our time and effort on the transactions that will actually increase our wealth, we spend it on finding jobs for ourselves.

Why we adopt this "work equals money" mentality is easy to understand. From the time we were little, we have lived with that idea.

Do some reflection. What was your initial position? For a neighbor, did you mow the lawn? After finishing the job, didn't you receive paid? You did, without a doubt. You were being compensated to cut grass, not to think.

You were paid to make hamburgers and French fries when you were older and obtained a job at the neighborhood burger business. Before being paid, you cooked the hamburgers and fries. Word really did equate to money.

You weren't being compensated by the proprietor of the hamburger establishment to discover a more effective method of preparing hamburgers or to search for a new outlet to sell them in. Only for the labor involved in preparing the hamburgers did he pay you.

However, the "job" you do today is not compensated. It's not your effort that's bringing in the cash.

However, you don't need to look for it because the work still needs to be done. You'll be found by it. Deals that will bring in money are what you should be searching for right now.

WHICH ELEMENTS MAKE UP WORK?

The definition of "work" The daily tasks that must be completed in order for a business to run are the only "work" that any business does.

It is necessary to return phone calls.

It is necessary to read and reply to emails. There must be order in the files. However, all of this is "work" and the list goes on and on.

You won't be paid for taking calls, reading emails, or organizing files. Simply put, that is "work" that needs to be done. It isn't bringing in any money for you, and it is unquestionably not what you should be concentrating on.

Paying a virtual assistant to handle the "job" once an internet marketing business is up and running is a very wise investment since it frees you up to negotiate deals that will bring in revenue and help your business grow.

Naturally, you can't accomplish this immediately, but you may try to spend as little time as possible on monotonous jobs.

You may labor on your website for hours on end, improving it by making small adjustments here and there. That kind of employment does not increase your bank account's balance in the slightest.

Hire a techie to handle that "job" for you while you close transactions that generate more than enough money to cover the techie's salary.

Get it mended as soon as you can, and then proceed to the fruitful deal-making, until you can engage someone to handle this work for you.

How long do you spend each day writing and publishing to your blogs? Does this time actually generate any revenue for you?

Naturally, the answer is no. Just "work," really. It is work that you may discover ways to outsource or shorten, for as by using PLR content rather than writing every word yourself.

The provision of excellent customer service is an important necessity. Fast, effective, and most importantly skilled execution are required.

It can even be work that, initially, you have to accomplish by yourself.

However, there are businesses and people in cyberspace who are more than capable of performing this task for you, so you don't have to make it more difficult than it needs to be.

WHAT QUALIFIES AS MAKING DEALS?

Undoubtedly, the "job" must be done, but it should be done as fast and effectively as possible. You shouldn't focus your efforts on looking for and producing additional unprofitable work.

Making deals that will bring in money should be your main priority.

To free up as much of your own time as possible for deal making, you should start hiring individuals as soon as you can to handle the menial duties that need to be completed.

What precisely constitutes deal-making actions then? Simply said, they are the pursuits that have the ability to add funds to your bank account. These include, among others:

1. Visiting niche-related forums and blogs: Forums and blogs are where you find the real, live, breathing people who are YOUR potential customers. Until someone pulls out their credit card, enters their information, and actually purchases goods or services from you, you haven't made a dime, so you need to go where the people are and figure out how to best meet their wants and needs.

2. Look up relevant websites to your own. Your possible partners for a joint venture can be found here. Make deals that will benefit both parties by contacting the webmasters.

3. Establish a newsletter or e-zine of your own. This is one of the most lucrative deals you can strike for yourself. The more your list expands, the more money you can earn.

4. Attend brick-and-mortar seminars and create strong professional ties with individuals in your industry. Again, they are possible joint venture partners that you should spend time cultivating.

5. Create a webinar or teleseminar on your own: Find speakers who would be intriguing to your list and who might provide them with knowledge. Both webinars and teleseminars may be done easily and cheaply, and both are profitable ventures.

DOES THIS IMPLY THAT WE SHOULD STOP WORKING AND CONCENTRATE SOLELY ON BUSINESS DEALS?

It would be so lovely if we could just stop working eight hours a day and spend all of our free time closing deals that will bring in cash! That is what I would consider a perfect world.

Unfortunately, we will likely have to handle both of these tasks until our "ship comes in" in addition to the day-to-day job that must be completed.

We can at least learn how to work more efficiently if we have to do both. We can learn how to complete the same amount of "work" in less time so that we have more time to pursue business opportunities that will increase our wealth.

Work smarter, for instance, by:

1. Create a FAQ page for your website and utilize your autoresponder to point visitors there with their queries.

2. Join a Private Label Rights (PLR) membership website and use the content there as your blog entries and website content (with only a little rewriting). Even whole new goods that you can sell can be created using this PLR content.

3. Create a schedule for yourself that allots a set amount of time to the necessary but money-making duties and more time to the deal-making tasks that will generate income.

4. Invest in automation software that is made to handle routine, but time-consuming, uncomplicated chores.

There is always "work" that needs to be done each and every day, but try not to let it consume all of your attention. Don't look for something to do. You are an internet marketer today, so work no longer means money.

Work as quickly as you can, and then concentrate on the deal-making tasks that will increase your revenue. Making hamburgers is no longer your only responsibility; you now also need to go out and hunt for new markets. You ARE currently being paid to think.

NOW IS YOUR CALL TO ACTION!

Your Internet business' success (or failure) really depends on you right now.

You will be solely responsible for your success or failure; the choice is yours. Your actions will determine whether you succeed or fail.

Both success and failure are equally important. Your own Internet business is the coin in question, and you don't want to toss it into the air and let chance determine whether it lands on success or failure.

You do have total control over the direction your Internet business takes, as you like.

Everything you decide will be up to you.

Making sensible decisions will allow you to succeed and achieve triumph.

Your online business will fail if you make poor decisions, and your aspirations and dreams will also burn up in the process.

CONQUERING THE ODDS

Of course, you are aware that your chances of success are slim. Thousands upon thousands of new online businesses are started every single day. 90% (ninety percent) of the internet enterprises that will be created today won't exist in 120 days.

That is accurate! Unless you can modify them, you have a 10% chance of truly succeeding with your online business. Those are not very good odds. Winning would be viewed as a long shot if it were a horse race.

That is the drawback, yet there is always an upside to everything.

The good news in this situation is that even if you only have a 10% chance of succeeding, you can significantly increase your chances by just adhering to the advice that has already been given.

By simply applying a few very basic ideas to the issue, you can raise your chances from 10% to 90%.

Four factors can be used to explain why so many new Internet entrepreneurs fail within the first 120 days.

1. They are not in the proper frame of mind.

2. They don't establish a firm basis.

3. They lack the key to unlock development and growth.

4. They don't make success plans.

THE IDEAL ATTITUDE FOR SUCCESS

Unfortunately, a lot of individuals believe they can quit their jobs, start an online business, and then simply kick back and enjoy life. They anticipate quick wealth and success without having to put any effort (not even time) into achieving it.

They genuinely think they can sleep till noon, work whenever and however they want, and just rake in the cash. At least half of all startup online enterprises fail as a result of this mentality.

An internet business requires a lot of time and effort to be successful.

Your attendance at that previous real-world work was required for at least 40 hours per week.

If you want your online business to succeed, you'll need to put in around twice that much time each week. Because so few people are prepared to put in that much time and effort, 90% of attempts fail.

The majority of the few who are prepared to invest the necessary time and effort hope for immediate success.

Even though those data arc easily available, they don't even take into account the reality that they will need to continue to pay their own personal expenses for many months before they see the first dime of profit from a new internet business.

These are the people who search the internet for quick money schemes and fall prey to online con artists.

The best frame of mind is this: You should anticipate working hard. You must anticipate working a lot of tedious hours. You won't become successful overnight. There won't be a line of people waiting to hand you money. You'll have to work for it.

BUILDING A STABLE FOUNDATION

On occasion, someone will launch an online business without having any prior business experience. This is yet another factor contributing to the high failure rate of new internet businesses.

You would be very sensible to consult folks who are knowledgeable about business if you lack a business degree.

Any form of online business is a business. It must be managed like a business and constructed using ethical business principles. The only inquiries that are "stupid" are those that are never posed.

The best method to obtain the information you require is to simply ask individuals who already know the answers questions.

On the internet and in the real world, there are courses available regarding how to launch and manage a successful business.

If you don't understand the rules, you can't follow them. Prepare for your business launch by doing your research.

To prevent your new company from being one of the victims of inadequate or even no preparation, you need to establish a rock strong foundation. A business plan is necessary.

You must have a business plan that you can comprehend and implement. It's not a strategy to just go in and hope for the best. That will only guarantee that your new online business won't still be around in four months.

UNLOCKING EXPANSION AND GROWTH

In this world, nothing ever remains the same. Change is the one thing that cannot change.

This restriction applies to businesses conducted online as well. In actuality, business on the internet is changing more quickly than you might think.

Another factor contributing to the short lifespan of so many new online firms is the tendency of new e-entrepreneurs to launch a company with just one idea and never grow or expand it past that one.

These individuals have what I sometimes refer to as "tunnel vision." They fail to take stock of the online business environment and make the necessary adjustments to stay competitive and visible.

If the owner or manager of the business develops and broadens his knowledge and is prepared to adapt to the inevitable changes that occur on a daily basis in Internet business, then Internet enterprises will naturally grow and expand.

To put at least 5% of your time and revenue back into yourself is just smart business. Your business IS YOU.

The phrase "continuous education" has been bandied about as if it were a decision to be made.

If a firm wants to succeed, it cannot opt out of continuing education. Owners or managers of the 10% of newly launched online firms who will still be in operation after the subsequent 120 days will be those who are constantly learning new skills and applying them to their own businesses.

Attending seminars about the real world. Teleseminars and webinars are attended by them. Every single day they read a number of newsletters.

They prosper because they learn, advance, and adapt. Despite how simple it is to say, doing so is far more difficult. Those who succeed will, however, continue to operate even when most others do not.

EFFECTIVE PLANNING

I frequently quote a proverb from long ago. Whoever doesn't plan, plans to fail. It is the most crucial aspect of success, in a nutshell, and I repeat it frequently.

The same way a road map would be used for a road trip, an internet business strategy is very similar to one.

It is a thorough strategy for traveling the shortest distance feasible and avoiding scenic routes between points A (beginning an online business) and B (running a successful online business).

Most often, persons who launch new online firms have been employed in salaried positions. They operate their online enterprises with the mentality that "labor equals money," as a result of their current state of mind.

In addition, rather of looking for ways to produce money, they will spend their time looking for additional "work" to perform.

Without a swift shift from the mentality that "labor = money" to "sales = money," the company will undoubtedly fail, and fail very soon.

A business plan should include the advice to "find a mentor" as one of its most crucial recommendations. Even if you have every single step of your success strategy planned out in detail, finding a mentor can speed up the process by a factor of two.

Of course, it is quite improbable that you will discover a mentor within the first 120 days of launching your new online business, but you should keep that possibility in mind while you network and develop professional connections.

Although it is a very exciting endeavor, starting an online business is not without its challenges. Although it won't be simple or quick, you can overcome the challenges and triumph. That won't happen.